HONDA

HONDA

Chris Myers

Arco Publishing, Inc. *New York*

Published by Arco Publishing, Inc.
215 Park Avenue South, New York, NY 10003

© Chris Myers 1984

All rights reserved. No part of this publication
may be reproduced, in any form or by any means,
without permission from the Publishers.

Library of Congress Catalog Card Number: 83-73618
ISBN 0-668-06166-9 Hardcover Edition
ISBN 0-668-06173-1 Paper Edition

Printed in Italy

Contents

1 *History*   7
2 *Road-going Lightweights*   15
3 *Road-going Middleweights*   28
4 *Road-going Bigger Bikes and Superbikes*   38
5 *Sporting Bikes*   51
6 *Star Riders*   59

Index   64

1 History

The Honda story is a classic tale of success. It is the story of one man, Soichiro Honda, and his unparalleled achievement of bringing motor cycles to the masses, and keeping them up-to-date so that they remain popular in this ever-changing world.

Today, the Honda Motor Company is by far the world's biggest motor-cycle maker, producing motor cycles for delivery boys, housewives, serious road riders thirsty for speed and performance and, of course, for World Championship racers in both road racing and moto cross.

How did this all come about? The answer is that Honda himself set out to design bikes that were right for the time and right for the people. He designed motor cycles for people who didn't think they even wanted to get on two wheels.

Honda's first motor cycle was born out of necessity in bomb-ravaged, immediate post – World War II Japan, where what public transport there was left was desperately overcrowded and petrol severely restricted.

Casting around for a solution to his, and thousands of others', personal transport problems, Honda came across a job lot of 500 war surplus two-stroke motors designed to run electric generators; nobody else wanted them so Honda picked them up cheap.

His aim was to adapt them for attachment to push-bikes and, by October 1946, his tiny plant in Hamamatsu was churning out complete, makeshift motor bikes using proprietary cycle frames. Because petrol was severely rationed, Honda adapted his motors to run on turpentine, a fuel that he himself distilled from pine trees and sold throughout Japan. Turpentine (or petrol eked out with turps) was hardly ideal for powering motor bikes, and anything up to 20 minutes' frantic pedalling was required to warm things up enough before you got underway.

Honda's first bikes were an instant success but, not surprisingly, supplies of the surplus engines ran out after only a few months. By then business was much too promising for Honda to switch from two-wheelers so he decided to manufacture his own motors. Using the surplus motor as his model, Honda designed and built his own 50cc unit within months and, in November 1947, the A-Type Honda was being manufactured and sold as a complete motor bike using bought-in cycle frames. Because this first ½ horsepower motor bike gave off such fumes and a stench of turpentine it has unkindly been dubbed the 'Chimney'.

overleaf: *One of Honda's earliest models, the C-Type was produced in 1949.*

In 1948 Honda produced a 90cc version – the B-Type – but the real milestone was to come the next year when the D-Type, 100cc two-stroke was manufactured. This was Honda's first proper motor cycle: it was designed and built as a complete machine and it used all Honda parts. This was a far cry from simply slotting a motor into a push-bike frame. Honda called his machine 'The Dream', because his dream of building a complete, efficient motor cycle had come true. But, as an engineer first and businessman second, Honda was pushed ever onwards to develop new machines. The Dream sold well, but Honda wanted to produce something more sophisticated.

This turned out to be the 146cc, four-stroke OHV E-Type Dream. A powerful machine developing 5½bhp, the new Dream was undergoing road trials in July 1951, less than three years after those first A-Types went into production. Now here was a 'real' motor cycle: the Dream was capable of 50mph, it didn't leak oil, it had a taut steel frame and proper suspension front and rear. By October the new Dream was in production to the tune of 130 units per day.

The following year Honda moved back into the real mass market and produced the first Cub – the F-Type. This was a ½ horsepower, 50cc, two-stroke unit that was produced in vast quantities: you could take one home to fit to your push-bike or buy the complete red and white Honda 'Auto Bai'. Less than a year after the launch, production was hitting 6500 units per month and that translated into 70 per cent of Japan's powered two-wheeler market at the time.

In 1953 Honda announced a 90cc, single, four-stroke machine of even more sophistication. This was the Benly – a Japanese word for 'convenience'. The Benly J-Type had a pressed-steel frame, a neat rear suspension system where both engine and swinging arm 'see-sawed' on a sprung pivot, telescopic front suspension and the 3.8bhp motor had a three-speed gearbox. Soon the Benly was selling 1000 a month.

A 200cc scooter, the Juno, was produced in 1954 to catch some of the sales of the Vespa scooter copies that were being built in Japan and, over the next three years, Honda produced different versions of the Dream and Benly machines incorporating different size engines (up to 350cc) and refinements (such as twin shock, swinging-arm, rear suspension in the 1955 Dream and Benly machines).

Honda's first twin-cylinder motor cycle, the C70 Dream – a 250cc four-stroke – was launched in Japan in September 1957. This sophisticated OHC machine was the forerunner of Honda's high-performance 125 and 250cc twins that were to spearhead their massive export successes to the U.S.A. and Europe two years later.

The most momentous announcement, though, came in 1958 when Honda launched in Japan what was destined to become the world's most successful motor cycle – the C100 Super Cub.

Soichiro Honda and his team worked for more than three years on the Super Cub in a bid to produce a cheap, practical motor cycle that literally anyone could use. Using a 50cc four-stroke OHV motor, a centrifugal clutch and three-speed transmission so easy to operate that novices could ride it as easily as a push-bike, the

By October 1951 the E-Type Dream was being produced at a rate of 150 units per day.

Super Cub was an instant success. Its innovative 'crossbar-less' frame made it popular with the ladies and it set a whole new trend in commuter motor cycling. In fact a new phrase – 'scooterette' – was coined to describe this 'step-through' style machine. Launched in July 1958 the Super Cub was an instant success. Less than five years later five million units (in 50, 70 and 90cc versions) had been built.

By 1974 ten million had been built and sold and today's figure is much higher. And proof of the 'rightness' of the original concept is the fact that today's C50, 70 and 90s have only detail changes to set them apart from the machines of 25 years ago.

Early in 1958 Honda fitted an electric starter to the 250cc Dream and named it the C71 and, the following year, the latest Benly – a 125cc OHC twin of incredible sophistication and capable of 70mph – was launched as the C92.

That same year, 1959 – coincidentally the same year as Honda first ventured to the Isle of Man TT races with his high-revving 125cc DOHC twin racers – Europe had their first close-up look at the Japanese threat to their established motor

11

The 1953 J-Type Benly. Benly is the Japanese word for 'convenience'.

cycle industries when the 250cc C72 Dream was launched in Amsterdam. This, the first Japanese bike to be shown officially in Europe, stunned show-goers with its sophisticated OHC all-aluminium engine, electric starter, unusual pressed-steel frame, swing arm and front leading link forks, and indicators.

The 250cc market at the time in the U.K. was ripe for the picking, as learners – a vast market – had just been restricted to this size of machine and wanted the fastest bikes they could ride legally. And the Hondas were the fastest 250s going: the C72, successor to the C71, was capable of 80mph, yet could still return 66 miles per gallon. A few of the C71s came to Britain, but big sales were reserved for the C72s with their improvements like 12-volt electrics and wet sump lubrication.

The C92 Benly 125s came to Britain first in 1960, and found a ready market despite their tiny size – both wheels were only 16in. in diameter!

Over the next few years the Benlys and Dreams were produced in different sizes and constantly refined. CB versions of the Benly and Dream were introduced in 1961 with improved performance. The CB92 retained the pressed-steel frame and leading link forks while the CB72 went

The 1958 C100 Super Cub was cheap, practical and easy to ride. It caught on immediately and was to become the world's most successful motor cycle.

over to a racy style tubular frame and telescopic front suspension. It is worth recalling that Honda prices were very competitive in the U.K. – £238.80 for the C72 and £283.60 for the CB72 in 1961.

A 154cc version of the Benly came in 1964 – the C95 – and a 161cc version – the CB160 – was also offered.

A 305cc version of the Dream – the C77 – came out in 1963 and the CB77 – a Super Sports machine with 28½bhp on tap – was launched later that year as the fastest (95mph) and most powerful production Honda ever.

Keen to cash in on the big bike market, Honda launched their innovative 43bhp CB450 twin in 1965. This was a double overhead-camshaft machine with torsion bar valve springs that would do a genuine 104mph – a machine to challenge the 500cc-plus British bikes.

The CB450 went on sale in Britain in February 1966 at £360, but despite the machine's performance, sales generally world-wide were poor and after a number of engineering changes and re-vamps (a five-speed gearbox was added in 1967), the bike had faded away by 1971.

For 1968 Honda withdrew the old CB72 and

13

CB77 and produced a new range of SOHC twins: the CB250 and CB350 both with five-speed gearboxes and high performance – the 350 could hit 106mph.

Honda, however, had not given up in the big capacity class – far from it. After months of tantalising rumour, they launched a machine that was so powerful and fast a new word had to be coined to describe it. The word, of course, was 'superbike', the bike, the CB750F four. The machine was launched at the Tokyo Show of 1968, and when it came to Britain in April 1969, it set the biking world alight. Performance was staggering: 120mph was easy and acceleration far better than anything on the road. A 500cc four followed in April 1971 and in 1974 was replaced with a 550cc version.

In the 1970s 250 and 350cc machines were constantly modified (as all Hondas were) to keep pace with developments . . . and fashion. Both were given disc brakes and the 350 eventually up-rated to 360cc. In April 1972 a beautiful 350cc SOHC four was introduced, the CB350F, which was never sold in Britain. We had to wait until 1975 when a 400cc version was finally brought to the U.K. and it was a bike that instantly found favour with riders across the board.

The same year a 500cc twin, the CB500T, reminiscent of the old CB450, went on sale in Britain. But it seemed fated from the start: it never really caught on and was dropped after less than three years.

1975 saw the launch of by far the most sophisticated Honda yet: the water-cooled, flat four GL1000 Gold Wing. Here was a touring bike that set new standards of stamina, comfort and sophistication. This bike had shaft-drive, all disc braking and a novel 4.8 gallon petrol tank under the seat to keep the weight low. The dummy 'petrol tank' concealed all the electrics.

In the 1970s Honda went into the off-road market for the first time with the two-stroke moto crosser – the Elsinore – that was sold in the U.S.A. in 1972. The following year trail versions, known as the MT125 and MT250, were sold in the U.S.A. Late in 1970 Honda launched a 'semi-serious', four-stroke trail bike – the SL125 four-stroke single – in Japan, and followed that with the more serious SL250 in 1972. The 250 had long travel suspension, bags of ground clearance and performed well both on- and off-road. In 1973 XL versions of both bikes were launched with much improved off-road performance.

In February 1970 Honda got into the three-wheeler off-road market with the ATC90. ATC stands for All Terrain Cycle and today there is a a range of six ATCs in the U.K.

In the mid 1970s Honda broke with tradition and produced a two-stroke road machine, a moped known as the Amigo. This proved cheaper to manufacture than the existing four-stroke machines and spawned a new generation of Honda lightweight, two-stroke mopeds.

For 1977 Honda announced totally new and re-styled CB250 and CB400 twins with novel three-valve cylinder heads to replace the ageing CB250 and 400 twins.

2 Road-going Lightweights

Honda's great strength has always been in their lightweight motor cycle range and to keep it selling well over the years they have operated a continual process of revisions and re-styling as tastes, habits and international legislation change.

At the very bottom end of the market the recent trend has been away from four-stroke machinery towards simple, two-stroke bikes. This has allowed Honda to offer mopeds, for example, with much more sophisticated features at lower prices. Today's lightweights mostly have 12-volt electrics, electric starting, and are easier than ever to ride and run. Scooters – 1980s style – are coming to the fore and the new 125cc Learner Laws in Britain have focused attention on this important class. Today's 125cc Hondas have features, such as electric-starting and disc brakes, normally only found on bigger bikes.

The 100/125cc OHC single that first appeared in 1970 now powers a whole range of road and trail bikes. And the OHC twin-motor, which made its debut in the 125cc Benly, has powered over the years a whole range of sports and commuter bikes.

One motor cycle though has resisted change over the years and today, in its many forms, is still a best-seller – the C50 scooterette. For years this machine has been available in 50, 70 and 90cc forms and the latter has for ages been the top-selling motor cycle in Britain. In some countries an electric-start version is on offer and in 1980 an 'Econopower' version of the 70 was launched with low-friction bearings and a special cylinder head to give much improved economy.

Today's range of Honda lightweights caters for every conceivable taste from bread-and-butter family commuting mopeds to 'state of the art' 125cc twins with disc brakes and the latest single rear shock Pro Link suspension. The U.K. range of up to 250cc road bikes is 37 strong!

Mopeds, Scooters and Step-throughs

With 16 mopeds on offer in 1983 Honda have an unrivalled choice in this sector catering for everyone, from non-motor-cycling types who want an easy-to-ride automatic, to 16-year-olds who are restricted to 30mph mopeds, but who want as much style as they can afford; there is even a novel, three-wheeler moped.

Back in 1977 Honda's moped range was being heavily infiltrated by two-strokes. The first two-stroker in the moped range – in the entire bike range for that matter – was the PF50MR2 Amigo in

above: *The NS50, launched in 1981 was Honda's contender in the expanding scooter-moped market.*

left: *The C50L scooterette is the successor to the C100 Super Cub. The 1981 model is shown here.*

overleaf: *The futuristically styled Stream moped is the most expensive ever, at £675.*

1975. (That's discounting, of course, those early two-strokes of the late 'forties and early 'fifties that never found their way out to the West.)

In 1978 Honda introduced their big-selling, two-stroke moped, the Express. Extremely cheap and easy to ride, with automatic oiling – a new feature – the Express sold like hot cakes, helped no doubt by an advertising campaign featuring the well-known model, Twiggy. Today it is the cheapest model in the range. It is available with single-speed or two-speed auto-transmission. It has small wheels and an open frame which appeals to women riders.

A big seller in 1977 was the two-stroke Camino which featured an infinitely variable V-belt

17

transmission. This bike had bigger wheels than the Express which made it a bit nippier on the road. Both were, and still are, capable of over 100mpg.

On the four-stroke front the old-fashioned pushrod-operated valve PF50 Novio and PX50K1 – successor to Honda's first international moped of the 'sixties – were still around, despite their relative lack of sophistication.

Star performer was the SS50 four-stroke sports moped. Introduced four years earlier in response to the new Learner Law that restricted 16-year-olds to mopeds, the SS50 had a tuned OHC motor and all but useless pedals. The law didn't specify any power for mopeds, only that they be 50cc and have pedals, so Honda tuned the bike to do 50mph! The SS50, though, was withdrawn at the end of 1977 and replaced with the CB50J moped when the law was changed to specify a power figure and dispensed with the old ruling on pedals.

The only moped around today with a four-stroke motor is the single seat C50L scooterette. Successor to the 1958 C100 Super Cub, the C50 has remained a strong seller over the years, and a fully automatic three-speed version, the C50LA, was launched in 1982.

The C50L has the conventional auto-clutch and semi-automatic, three-speed transmission, whilst the C50LA has the new all-automatic, three-speed transmission. Both offer weather protection and both will do a minimum of 100mpg.

Honda got into the expanding scooter-moped market with the NS50 Melody – a two-stroke – in 1981 and one version, the DeLuxe, came later,

with an electric starter. Another variation on the same theme, the Caren, was launched the same year. This is a model designed to appeal to the ladies, and Honda have three variations in their range for 1983.

1980 saw a futuristic new moped, the MB50, a two-stroke with up-to-date bike styling and big-bike features, such as a front disc brake. The MBX50 is top of the moped range for 1983. It is a sporty, six-speed two-stroke with Pro Link rear suspension and front disc brake. An unrestricted 80cc version is also on offer – the MBX80. There is also an enduro-styled version – the MTX50.

Introduced in 1982 the three-wheeler Stream moped has a swing frame that keeps the rear wheels vertical as you lean through corners. It is fully automatic and is futuristically styled. It is easily the most expensive moped ever, at £675.

There are four unrestricted step-throughs in the U.K. range and all rely upon the little four-stroke powerplant that made its debut in the C100 of 1958. Today all are OHC (the C100 had pushrod-operated valves) but the power units in C50, C70, C90 and CF70 are all very much the same motors as pioneered in the C100 more than 25 years ago.

Today the C70 has a 're-engineered' motor with low friction rings and bearings, together with a new design of cylinder head that allows a high compression to be used with low octane petrol. The result is a low mpg motor christened 'Econopower'. The CF70 is physically the smallest step-through with tiny 10in. wheels.

The 1981 Lead, often considered as Honda's first proper scooter since the early Juno.

Using an enlarged version of the MBX motor is the H100. With a more conventional frame, lacking the MBX's Pro Link, the H100 has a drum brake at the front and is envisaged as a budget commuting bike, but with 11.5bhp on tap it's a lively performer.

Many would regard the 80cc two-stroke Lead to be Honda's first proper scooter since the early Juno. A joy to ride, with its all-automatic transmission, the Lead has an electric starter that will not engage unless a brake is on – this is designed to stop you racing off unexpectedly!

Two other scooters are new for 1983. There's a 125cc version of the Lead with a bigger two-stroke motor and the CH125 scooter – a four-stroke with water-cooling. Known as the Spacy, the CH125 is claimed to be Honda's most economical 125cc machine and will do over 150mpg. A novel idea is a warm-air ducting system from the radiator which keeps your feet warm in cold weather!

One of Honda's five 125cc 'learner' bikes for 1983, the XL125R, is a trail bike with Pro Link rear suspension.

Apart from the H100 only one other 100cc machine is imported into the U.K. – the CB100 roadster.

This uses the well-proved and bullet-proof SOHC four-stroke motor that is essentially the same as the power plant in the 125cc single-engined Hondas.

The MTX125R is restricted to 12bhp in Britain, but in France it is claimed to develop 24bhp.

The 125cc Range

After years of producing 125cc OHC twins Honda came up with an OHC single of almost the same horsepower in 1972 – the 14bhp CB125S. This proved extremely popular as it was capable of nearly 70mph and fuel consumption that rarely dropped below 100mpg. That power unit has remained pretty well unchanged to this day and powers the XL125 trail bike, launched in 1975. A budget 125 single with pushrod-operated valves – the CG125 – was launched in 1976.

Successor to the famous Benlys of the 'sixties, the CB125T OHC twin of 1977 was a powerful machine developing around 15bhp and capable of more than 70mph. Unlike the Benly, the 125T had a single front disc brake and in 1978 was equipped with alloy wheels. When the 12bhp ruling was introduced in 1982 Honda dropped the 125T and replaced it with an emasculated version that *looked* much faster, with modern styling and single-shock rear suspension – the CB125T-D Super Dream.

Eight 125cc so-called 'learner' bikes are in Honda's U.K. range for 1983 (not including the scooters) and all are restricted to 12bhp. Five are single-cylinder four-strokes: the XL125S and XL125R trail bikes; the new sporty-looking CB125RS; the CT125 designed for farm use; and the CG125 budget commuter introduced in 1976 is unique in that it's Honda's only pushrod-operated single-cylinder OHV machine. The difference between the two trail bikes is the provision of Pro Link rear suspension and different styling on the R model. Both have six-speed gear boxes, but naturally the R model is more expensive. The CB125RS is new for 1983 and has a front disc brake and styling similar to the CB250RS single.

Completely new for 1983, and exciting in that it's a high-performance, water-cooled two-stroke styled exactly like the works moto crossers, is the MTX125RW. This has Pro Link rear suspension, a big radiator with cowling and a seat that climbs up the tank – it looks just like the new CR125 moto

Top of Honda's 1983 125cc range, and the most expensive model, is the CB125T.

crosser. In the U.K. this is restricted to 12bhp, but in France, where they have different Learner Laws, it is claimed to develop 24bhp! In a sense, this bike is more sophisticated than the scrambler in that it has a mechanism to vary the exhaust expansion chamber size according to engine speed. This gives a much improved mid-range power response, but it is removed from the U.K. version. A 200cc version – the MTX200 – is also available.

The other 125s are all OHC four-stroke twins and can trace their lineage back to those early CB92s and C92s. All have single overhead-camshafts and basically the same motor.

The CD125 Benly is the budget commuter twin, and with a single carburettor and plain styling it's the cheapest too.

Custom fans are catered for with the CM125, essentially a tarted up Benly with fat rear tyre, two-step seat and high bars. Both the last two have four-speed gearboxes.

Top of the 125cc range for 1983 – as it was in 1982 – is the CB125TB. A direct descendant of the old and long-lost 15bhp 125SS of 1969, the new machine is completely restyled and re-engineered for the 1980s' youngsters. A tubular frame has Pro Link rear suspension, there are Comstar wheels, an electric starter, 12-volt electrics and, unlike the other twins, a five-speed gearbox. Looks are very tasty indeed. The CB125T is the most expensive 125 in Honda's range.

The 200cc Range

The mainstay of the genuine motor-cycle commuting market for years has been the CD series of OHC twin-cylinder machines. Starting out as the CD175 in the late 'sixties its successor was a big seller in 1977. The bike was sold as a plain, no-frills commuter with single carburettor and a pressed-steel frame. The drive chain was enclosed for low maintenance and 70mph could be maintained whilst enjoying fuel consumption in the low seventies mpg.

Over the last five years the CD has been enlarged, first to 185cc in 1978, and then to 200cc in 1979. 12-volt electrics and a five-speed gearbox (up from four) were added later. The bike today is a bit faster (it will reach the mid-seventies mph) and is still extremely frugal with petrol. It will return 90mpg in mixed running while still able to keep up with all traffic. Brakes are drums front and rear.

A custom version – the CM200T – is also available: it is a little more expensive and a little lighter at 269lb, but it's not quite so thrifty.

The 1973 version of the CD175, designed as a down-to-earth commuter, was later to be enlarged to 200cc and is still on the market today.

27

3 Road-going Middleweights

The 250cc Range

Honda's first 250cc twin was the C70 of 1957, but British bikers had their first brush with this sophisticated OHC machine when the electric start C71 was first imported in 1960. Late in 1960 the C72 250 became available; much improved, it had 12-volt electrics and wet-sump lubrication.

The 250s sold well, especially in Britain, latterly as the CB250, and in 1977 Honda decided to launch a sportier machine to recoup some of the ground they'd lost to other Japanese factories who were offering high-performance two-strokes. The result was the CB250T with a three-valve head (two inlet, one exhaust), short stroke motor producing 27bhp and revving to over 10,000rpm. It was a little heavy – 380lb – and tall, but handled well. It had a front disc brake and was capable of 90mph.

In 1978 Honda introduced their Eurostyling concept of integrating the tank, sidepanels and seat into one flowing line and re-styled the CB250 into the CB250N Super Dream. It was only a cosmetic change, but it ensured that the sales rocketed. The bike is still around today with styling changes – Comstar wheels (spoked type made from pressed steel) were added in 1979, and it has been top of the full-sized bike sales charts in the U.K. for years.

Currently Honda have two versions of this bike in their range: the CB250 Super Dream Deluxe and the custom CM250. Both have the same six-speed, counterbalanced 249cc, 27bhp motor featuring a three-valve head that means 90mph can be achieved. Both, too, are extremely well-equipped – the CB has matt black pressed-steel Comstar wheels, electric starter and all the usual accompaniments. The CM is seven pounds heavier, has a longer wheelbase, lower gearing and the smaller 16in. rear wheel is complemented by an 18in. instead of a 19in. front wheel. It's a little slower and thirstier.

The innovative four-valve head, OHC, single 250cc motor that made its debut in 1972 in the XL250 trail bike has powered this machine over the last eight years with no serious changes. An automatic decompressor linked to the kickstart to improve starting came in 1979, and the motor was put in a road frame to create the 1980 90mph CB250RS, whose four-valve head was complemented by twin exhaust ports and pipes.

These features, plus an extremely short stroke motor, mean that this unit produces a healthy

Based on the 1972 XL250 trail bike motor, the CB250RS is an exciting bike to ride and is very popular in the U.K.

26bhp – just the same as the twins. Of course, the whole bike is lighter than the twins by 85lb, and that means it is quicker by around 5mph. You'll get five more mpg too. An electric starter is standard and the kick starter is linked to an automatic exhaust valve decompressor to make starting easier. A much more exciting bike to ride, the RS has become much loved in the U.K.

An incredible success in Japan during 1982, and now sold in the U.K., is the innovative VT250 – a DOHC, water-cooled, 90-degree v-twin. The VT has four valve combustion chambers, a six-speed

above: The VT250F is now being sold in the U.K. after its incredible success in 1982 in Japan.

right: The long-serving XL250 trail bike still retains its popularity.

gearbox and a hydraulic clutch – a feature normally found only on bigger bikes. With 35bhp on tap at 11,500rpm it's capable of 100mph and has already been earmarked as a production racer. The frame is the latest twin loop type and rear suspension is Pro Link. At the front there's an anti-dive device to stop the forks compressing

on braking. Front and rear brakes are the very latest inboard ventilated discs that are designed to keep the rain off the mechanism. Its dry weight is light at 328lb.

When the rumours began flying around that Honda planned a 250cc two-stroke triple, no one believed them. But now there is such a bike – the v-three MVX250. Water-cooled, with a 90-degree cylinder angle, this bike is obviously built from experience gained on the NS500 racer. But the configuration is different – instead of one cylinder forward and two up, this bike has two cylinders forward and one up. Power output is 40bhp, making it Honda's most powerful, and certainly their fastest, 250 ever. It's been timed at 110mph! Designed to compete head on with Yamaha's RD250LC water-cooled twin, the MVX has all race-type gear such as the latest style twin loop frame, but sadly will not be sold in Europe or the U.K. in 1983.

Honda's other 250s are trail bikes: the XL250R and CL250. The 1983 XL250 is as good today as it has always been – better in fact. Kitted out with the counterbalanced 250cc, four-valve, OHC motor giving 22bhp at 8000rpm, today's XL has the refinement of Pro Link rear suspension and many enduro-type features, including quick-release hubs that make it a serious off-road iron. It's also quite at home on the road. Today's 250 has conventional 21in. diameter front wheels and a 17in. rear – in the late 1970s a 23in. front wheel was used because, Honda claimed, this improved steering characteristics. In 1981 they reverted to the conventional size – it seemed the benefits weren't that wonderful.

A new inclusion in the 1982 British range was the CL250 trail bike. Based upon the 1981 'Pre-Pro Link' XL engine and chassis, the CL has an upswept exhaust, electric starter and an extra low 'crawler' first gear. Seen as a sort of luxury trail bike, in the mould of Honda's early CL250 twin machine of the late 'sixties, the bike has so far failed to catch the British public's imagination.

The 300-400cc Range

Launched in 1963 the 305cc, OHC twins, the sporty CB77 and touring C77, filled an important place in the market for the more experienced riders. Both were withdrawn at the end of 1967 to pave the way for the new Dream, the CB350. Enlarged to 360cc in 1974, the bike sold well, especially in the U.S.A., where marketing studies showed that it was the middleweight most riders would buy. The 360 benefited from a six-speed gearbox and a disc front brake, but the extra capacity didn't result in any more power – it was used just to broaden the power band. Top speed was around 95mph.

The 1977 model was the CJ360 which reverted to a five-speed gearbox and had just a few styling changes as Honda tried to make it more appealing due to flagging sales. But no one really felt that any of the 360cc bikes had the same appeal as the 350s.

A whole host of 350-500cc fours appeared in the early 1970s ushered in with the CB500 of 1971

The CB400F, capable of 104mph, was an instant success when launched in 1977.

When the CB400 four went out of production, British riders turned to the VF400 four as a replacement, but this bike is 16bhp more powerful than its predecessor.

and quickly followed by the CB350 (never sold in the U.K.), and the CB400F of 1975. All used a similar motor built by Honda from experience gained on the CB750, but these smaller bikes were much more compact with a vertical block.

By 1977 the CB500 had been replaced with a 550cc version and British bikers could also buy the 105mph CB400F and the brand-new CB400T twin, basically an enlarged version of the three-valve CB250 launched at the same time, but much more exciting to ride. The CB400F became an instant success in Britain; it performed extremely well and, because of its handling qualities, was taken up by many production racers. It had a six-speed gearbox and was a delight to ride. And at 375lb it was light, too.

Surprisingly, the 400T proved almost as fast as the CB400F it was ultimately to replace. Honda gave the T model counterbalance shafts for smoothness, and it got sales they wanted.

The CB400 twin of 1983 is a 104mph machine that has found favour with one bike racing school

The quiet CX500, which ran on low-lead petrol, was brought out in 1978 in anticipation of the new regulations on noise and pollution.

in Britain. Only eight pounds heavier than the 250 at 381lb, the 395cc bike produces 43bhp and is a real performance machine. Like the 250, it has a six-speed gearbox, but up front it has twin disc brakes.

Ever since the demise of the much-loved CB400 four, British bikers have been looking to Honda for a replacement. Now they have it in the form of the v-four VF400. With a fantastic 53bhp available at 11,500rpm, this bike is 16bhp more powerful than the old CB400. The v-four motor has DOHC and is virtually a miniaturised version of the VF750 superbike launched in 1982. Frame and running gear are just like the VT250.

The 500 and 550cc Range

In 1978 Honda launched a bike that was a premonition of what bikers would be riding as restrictive noise and emission regulations really began to bite towards the end of the twentieth century. It was the CX500 – a bike with an extraordinary water-cooled, 80-degree, v-twin motor set across the frame and with four valve heads.

It was quiet, ran on low-lead petrol and had a maintenance-free shaft-drive. Unusually, the valves were operated by pushrods and the heads set at a skew angle on the barrels so that the carburettors could be tucked away. It was technically a difficult bike to design and there were a number of early problems with the timing chain and the cams themselves. But Honda stuck with it and the bike became the best-seller in its class in the U.K. It proved pretty fast for its 460lb weight, 110mph being attainable. A custom version was added in 1980, but this is no longer imported into Britain.

In 1979 Honda launched their biggest single-cylinder bike ever – the XL500 four-stroke. With 30bhp available from the SOHC four-valve motor, the XL proved to be a potent trail bike and the chassis, with its long travel suspension, made both on- and off-road riding easy. For 1982 Honda fitted the same motor, though with an electric starter, into the FT500 – a roadster, styled much like the American dirt track racers.

The CB550 four was dropped in 1979 to make way for a 650cc version, Honda apparently feeling that there was little world-wide support for the 550cc class. That may have been the case, but in 1980 interest in fast 550s really began to take off. Yamaha's XJ550 of 1981 was a runaway best-seller with its 110mph-plus performance and acceleration equal to several 750s.

So it was no surprise then when Honda launched a totally new 550 – the CBX550 – for 1982. It appears that development on this bike must have begun shortly after the demise of the 'old' CB550 – perhaps their engineers foresaw the expansion in this sector of the market. Actually a 572cc machine, this 123mph, 65bhp lightweight has already earned a reputation as the hottest 550cc bike on the market.

The new CBX has a DOHC motor with the alternator tucked behind the cylinders for a narrower plot, 16 valves, double overhead-cams and its all-up weight is just 405lb. Inboard floating discs are the stoppers on this innovative machine, and the Pro Link rear suspension is complemented by telescopic front forks that feature the latest hydraulic anti-dive systems.

There is an F2 version with skimpy fairing (13lb heavier), and in some countries, notably France, there is a 400cc version with single front disc. This is 399cc and it produces 48bhp.

New to Honda's 1982 range was the FT500, four-stroke, single roadster. A complete departure for Honda, this bike, styled after the dirt track racers of the American scene, has high handlebars, long-travel front forks, fat tyres and a box section swinging arm. Brakes are single discs front and rear and the two-into-one competition style matt black exhaust exits on the right-hand side (flat trackers circulate anti-clockwise).

The engine is a modified version of the four-valve, twin exhaust port XR500 enduro mill, but has an electric starter. For road use the FT gets a new 43mm constant vacuum carburettor. The end result is a machine that is light (345lb), handles well, goes well and stops well – only the fuel consumption at 52mpg disappoints.

The 1983 VT500 may not appeal visually to everyone, but it is relatively simple to ride and economic to run, which must make it popular.

New for 1983 was the 'fore-aft' v-twin VT500. This is not really designed as an out and out sportster and its 52-degree motor features three-valve combustion chambers and twin spark plugs for better economy and driveability. In the U.S.A. a custom-styled version is available, called the Shadow. Maximum power is claimed to be 50bhp. Styling isn't immediately attractive to the eye, but its relative simplicity and economy should make it appealing to many bikers. Final drive is by a shaft system.

4 Road-going Bigger Bikes and Superbikes

For 1983 Honda boosted the size of all their cx bikes to 650ccs. The most basic version is the E model (E for Eurosport) with sporty nose fairing and long seat; there's a touring version with screen and fairing – the Silver Wing – and of course there's the Turbo.

All the latest cx models have single shock Pro Link rear suspension and handle extremely well despite their slightly heavy stance – the Eurosport weighs 460lb dry. The Eurosport will do 120mph with ease and return fuel consumption in the mid-fifties.

The CB650SC Nighthawk is an attractive, not overdone, custom version of the old faithful four which dates back to 1978. This engine is the old twin valve job developed from the CB500 of a few years ago. It's supposed to be a custom bike, but actually looks quite good with colour matched frame, lots of chrome and long travel front air forks. It's very smooth, but it is interesting to compare its power output of 63bhp with the 65bhp of the up-to-the-minute CBX550.

Despite its capacity of only 673cc, the CX650 Turbo deserves inclusion in the superbikes chapter. In 1983 Honda increased the capacity of the old 497cc mill to 673 by boring and stroking it to 82.5 x 63mm. A re-programmed computer gives more low-and mid-range power to get this 517lb bike smartly off the line and, with maximum power up to a genuine 100bhp, the turbo should now be capable of over 130mph. The machine handles well and the turbo gives a real boost once 'on song', so that roll-on acceleration is more than a match for many 1000cc bikes. The bike has an anti-dive front end and a neat plastic fairing that is designed as part of the machine.

Towards the end of 1982 Honda launched two totally new shaft-drive fours in the U.S.A., both featuring adjustment-free hydraulic valve lash compensators. The bikes are known as the semi-custom styled CB650 and 550SC Nighthawks, not to be confused with the 'old' Nighthawk still sold in Europe. The new 650 has excelled itself in performance tests in the U.S.A., and no wonder, with 72bhp on tap and a low weight of 434lb dry. Sadly, this machine is not available in the U.K.

The 750cc Range

It's difficult for anyone under 30 years old to appreciate the enormous impact Honda's launch of their CB750 four in 1968 had. The bike was so big, so fast and so powerful a new word had to be coined for it: superbike.

When this 737cc machine was first tested by the Motor Cycle Magazine tester Dave Dixon he reported that the bike accelerated like nothing he'd ever experienced. He recorded a quarter mile time of 12.6 seconds and 102mph – top speed was 118mph. 'One of the most outstanding machines I've ridden', he concluded. It was also one of the heaviest at 491lb ready to ride. Sixty-seven brake horsepower was on tap – ten more than the recently announced British Triumph Trident. So, as well as blasting all opposition into the weeds and spawning a whole generation of copy-cat superbikes, the CB750 sounded the death knell for what remained of the British bike industry.

The engine was a single overhead-camshaft four using four carburettors. The gearbox housed five ratios and like most Hondas (and unlike the opposition) an electric starter was standard. Something else that set it apart from the opposition was the single front disc brake. The

A late version of Honda's CB650 four.

The turbo version of the CX650 is capable of 130mph and is more than a match for many 1000cc bikes.

full duplex frame, and more than adequate suspension, ensured that the bike handled well too, and it was rapidly taken up in production and endurance racing.

In 1970 American Dick Mann took a race-tuned CB750 to victory in the Daytona 200-mile race and one won the 1972 Belgian 24-hour endurance race at Liège.

The CB750 quickly became the most successful big bike ever: more than a million have now been sold. As proof that the bike was right from the start, Honda made few changes, other than styling ones, to this machine in its ten-year production span. It was given a bigger (3.9 gallon) petrol tank and other styling changes in 1971, when it became known as the K1, and given more warning lights a year later, when it became known as the K2.

In 1976 Honda introduced the CB750F1 with a four-into-one exhaust system instead of the old four separate pipes set-up and a rear disc brake. Other styling changes, such as a more angular tank, brought the bike well up to date in looks.

A much more worthwhile set of changes to the CB750 came in 1977 when the F2 version was announced with a whole series of tuning modifications such as bigger valves, higher lift cams and carburettors fitted with accelerator pumps that brought power output up to 69bhp at 8500rpm to make it more than competitive with the ever-increasing superbike competition. An important modification was the addition of a second front disc brake to improve stopping. A version with different paintwork and other detail styling changes – the K7 – was introduced in 1977 as a cheaper alternative.

A completely new machine with double overhead camshafts and four valve combustion chambers – the CB750KZ – was launched in 1978 to replace the ten-year-old SOHC model. The old CB750F2 and K7 models were still being sold off in Europe, however, until mid-way through 1979. The KZ was developed directly from the mid-seventies, European endurance championship-winning works Hondas. The bike had square bore and stroke dimensions of 62 x 62mm, giving a true displacement of 748cc – 9cc more than the old bike. With 79bhp on tap it was much more powerful, but it was heavy too (540lb), and many testers criticised its poor handling qualities. But it was fast for a 750 (120mph) and acceleration was excellent.

In 1980 the bike gained needle roller swing-arm bearings in place of the old plastic bushes that were not really up to the job, stronger front fork tubes with air-assistance and new rear dampers. An extra 2bhp, thanks to a new and less restrictive exhaust system, helped the top speed a little. Testers all over the world reported that now the handling matched the performance.

Today's water-cooled VF750S v-four is a fast motor cycle, capable of over 120mph. Despite its complex water-cooled motor and shaft-drive, and all its sophisticated instrumentation that incorporates a stop-watch and clock, it is just about the same weight as the CB750. A sports version is now available with chain, instead of shaft-drive – the VF750F. Much lighter, at 480lb dry, this ultra-short stroke motor is tuned to produce 90bhp and is capable of 130mph-plus.

Developed along the same lines as the FWS1000 Daytona racer, the motor has a unique one-way clutch built into the transmission to stop the rear wheel locking on heavy engine braking, a hydraulic clutch and race-style box section frame tubing. The front 16in. wheel (like the racers) has an anti-drive mechanism in the suspension and a Pro Link set-up is fitted at the rear.

The 900cc Range

Early in 1979 the CB900FZ was launched. Perhaps more than the 750 this bike owed its origins to the near 1000cc endurance racing Hondas. General specifications were exactly the same as the 750, but bigger bore and stroke dimensions of 64.5 x 69mm meant that the bike developed 95bhp and was capable of over 120mph. Front forks got air assistance in 1980 and in 1981 dual piston brakes were fitted front and rear – as they were on the 750.

The 1983 CB900F is little changed. Front forks get the new anti-dive system and the brakes are

41

the very latest twin-piston type. Power output remains a very competitive 95bhp and that makes it capable of a good 130mph with acceleration to match. Dry weight is claimed to be 532lb; that's up on the original weight but reflects the addition of the complex anti-dive mechanism and new brake calipers. A faired version, the F2, is available for a little extra cash.

above: *A close-up of the instrument panel on the pre-1983 CX500 Turbo.*

below: *The F2 version of the CB750, introduced in 1977, brought the model up to date, and made it more competitive with rival superbikes.*

42

1000cc and Above

In 1981 Honda launched the superbike that no one had predicted – a turbo-charged version of the cx500. A great deal of ballyhoo surrounded the launch and many claims were made for the machine: it was supposed to be more economic yet give the same sort of performance as a 1000cc machine, they said. A pity really, for though the reality was somewhat less wonderful, the cx500 Turbo was still an impressive machine. Top speed of around 125mph was the equal of machines displacing 250cc more and its top gear acceleration was more than a match for many 1000cc machines.

The bike was packed with electronics and a computer controlled the fuel injection system and ignition timing. Unlike the 'old' cx it had Pro Link rear suspension and anti-dive front forks. Handling was good, but it was very top-heavy. Fuel consumption was a disappointing 30mpg.

New for 1983 was the VF750F, which was much lighter and at least 10mph faster than the earlier bike.

overleaf: *The CBX1000, first produced in 1978, updated in 1981 and phased out in 1982, was the fastest ever production bike off the line.*

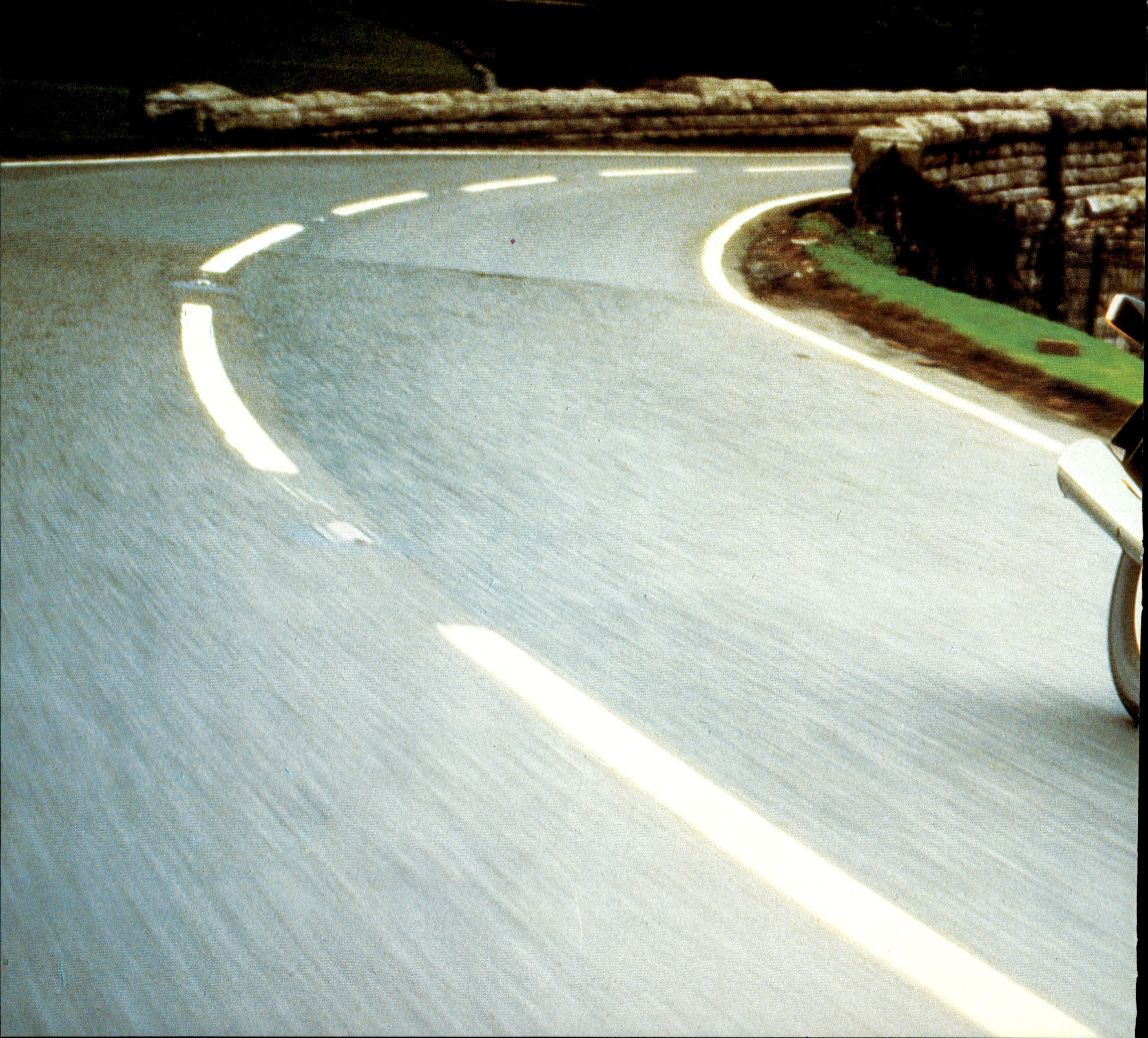

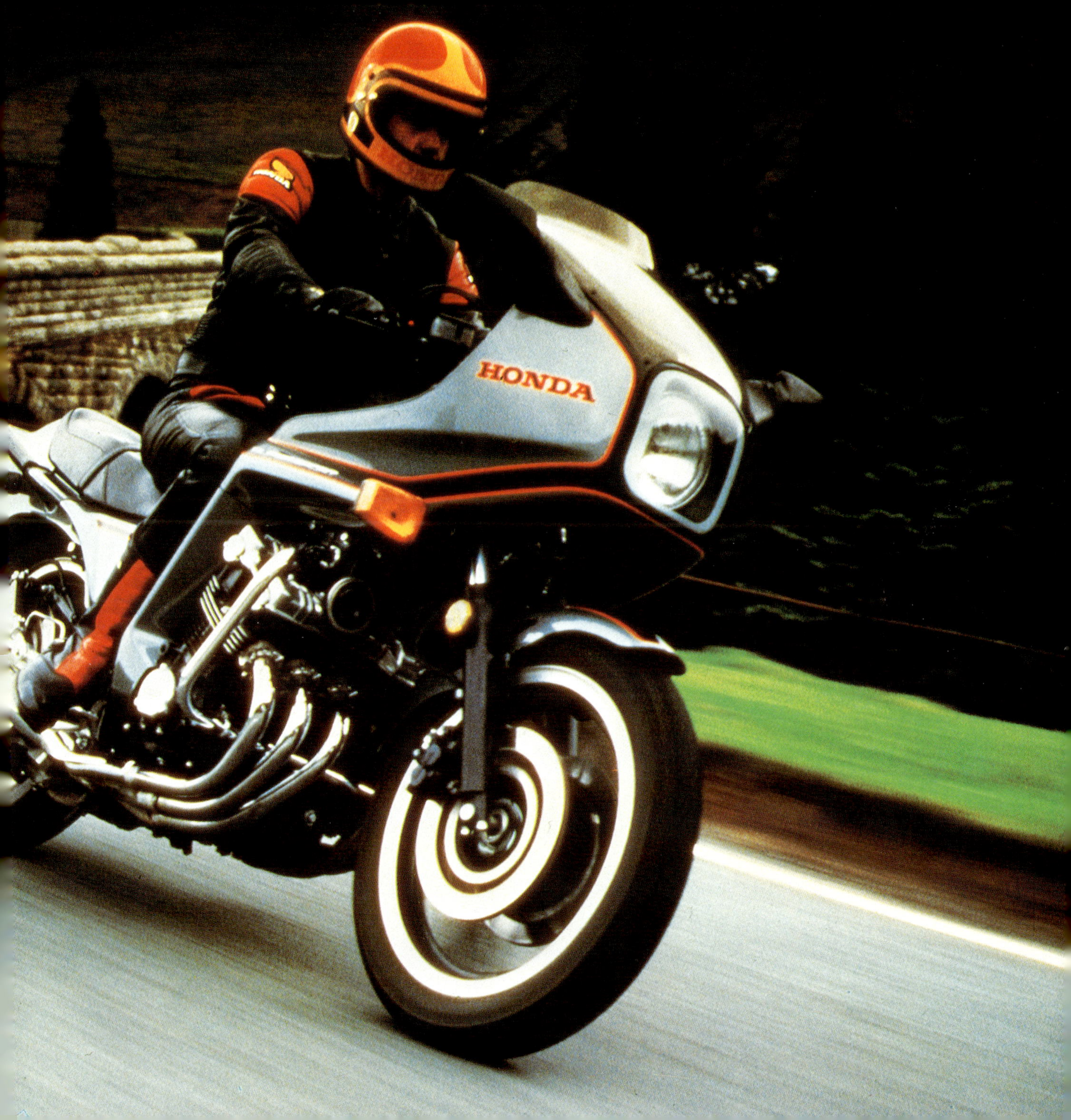
HONDA

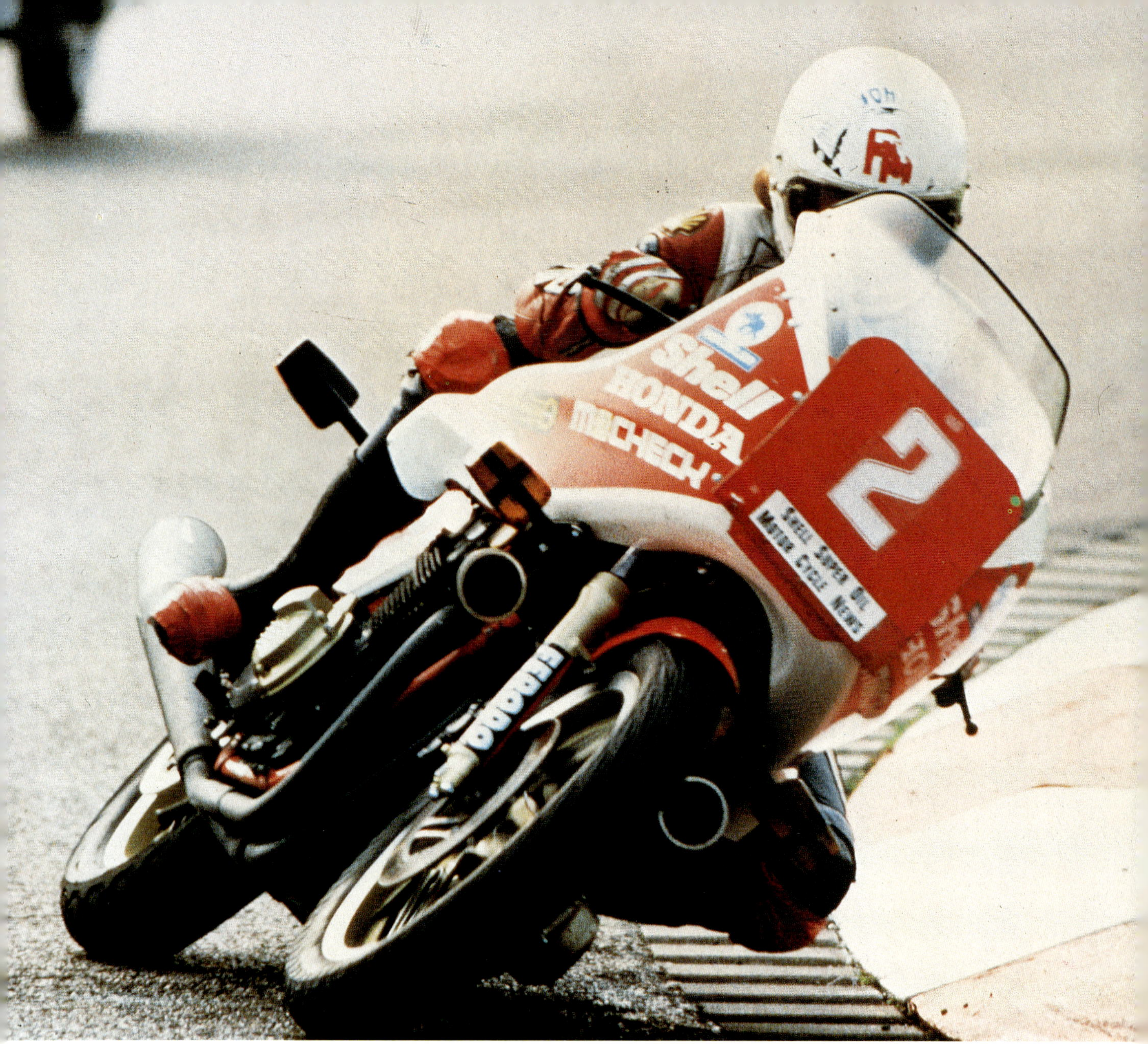
Shell
HONDA
2
Shell Super Oil
Motor Cycle News

The current range features the CX650 Turbo, if you want something expensive, exclusive and different.

Clearly based on Honda's 250cc six of the 1960s, the awesome 1047cc CBX six of 1978 was the most outlandish Honda ever produced. With 108bhp on tap this was an exercise in 'look what we can do' showmanship. Big and capable of close on 140mph, with its turbine-smooth 105bhp motor, the bike pushed back the frontiers of performance, but attracted criticism of its high-speed handling.

In 1981 the bike was given a much stronger single shock Pro Link rear suspension system and racing type ventilated disc brakes; it now handled beautifully, but weight was up to almost 600lb – partly due to the small fairing which came as standard. This was Honda's first, and only, six-cylinder roadster but sadly it failed to sell anywhere in sufficient numbers for Honda to justify its production. Production ceased late in 1982, although a few bikes were still on sale in 1983. Despite the fact that this bike was rather neglected by Honda's technicians as they concentrated on other new models in later years it's still the fastest production bike off the line – though its quarter-mile times are no better than, say, the CB900.

A 140mph hand-built version of the CB900 displacing 1085cc – the CB1100R – was launched in 1981 as a limited-run production road racer. In the hands of racers all over the world the bike

The CB1100R launched in 1981 won many championships round the world; this is Honda rider Ron Haslam racing one.

won championships with ease. But its annual production run of just a few hundred and its £4750 price tag limited it to a handful of enthusiasts and racers.

Honda call their 140mph CB1100R 'Ultra Sports' and that's just what this 120bhp machine is. With a motor derived from the CB900, but bored to 70mm from 54.5 this is a hand-built bike that's only available in extremely limited numbers; naturally most go to racers. Careful use of light alloys and plastics has allowed the weight to be kept at a competitive 512.6lb dry, almost 20lb lighter than the 900, and the 1100 comes with its own full race-type fairing. The amazing rear gas-charged shocks have 60 damping adjustments!

If the CB750 ushered in a new era for performance biking then the Gold Wing did the same for touring motor cycling when it was launched in 1975. Here was a bike with a unique specification: a flat four engine with twin camshafts, water-cooling, four carburettors, 4.8 gallon fuel tank under the seat and three disc brakes. Its engine configuration was the first flat four bike for 25 years and its 999cc motor was housed in a vast steel frame. Weight ready to roll was a massive 600lb. The motor churned out an average 83bhp and was surely the quietest ever made. Top speed was 120mph and the bike did just what Honda expected it to – sell in satisfying numbers to the long-distance touring, serious bikers. Changes over the years were very few and far between: in 1977 the old black exhaust with chrome side panels was replaced with an all-chrome offering, and in 1979 a more powerful Halogen headlamp and a new water temperature gauge were fitted. The biggest change came in 1980 when the motor was bored out to 1085cc: a move that increased the power a little, to 85bhp, and upped the already impressive torque figure. Air assisted suspension was also provided front and rear.

Today, if long-distance touring is your forte, then there are three variously equipped 1100cc Gold Wing machines available.

The most basic is the plain GL1100 – a naked bike with no kind of fairing. There's the faired GL1100D and the Aspencade version with just about everything. This, Honda's heaviest bike at 697lb dry (!), has fairing, top box, panniers and even an optional stereo radio and intercom. In America you can get a custom-fitted CB radio. Front and rear braking systems are linked for easy, powerful stopping and an onboard compressor allows you to pump up the front or rear suspension to compensate for added loads, or even if you spot a bumpy road ahead. It is Honda's second most expensive machine after the CB1100R.

Extraordinary Superbikes

Four extraordinary superbikes that are sold in the U.S.A. and elsewhere, but which won't be coming to Britain are the V65 Magna V-four, the CB1100F, the CB1000C and the VT750F.

The V65 is a massive 1100C version of the

An early example of the Gold Wing GL1000 for long-distance touring. In 1980 the motor was bored out to 1085cc.

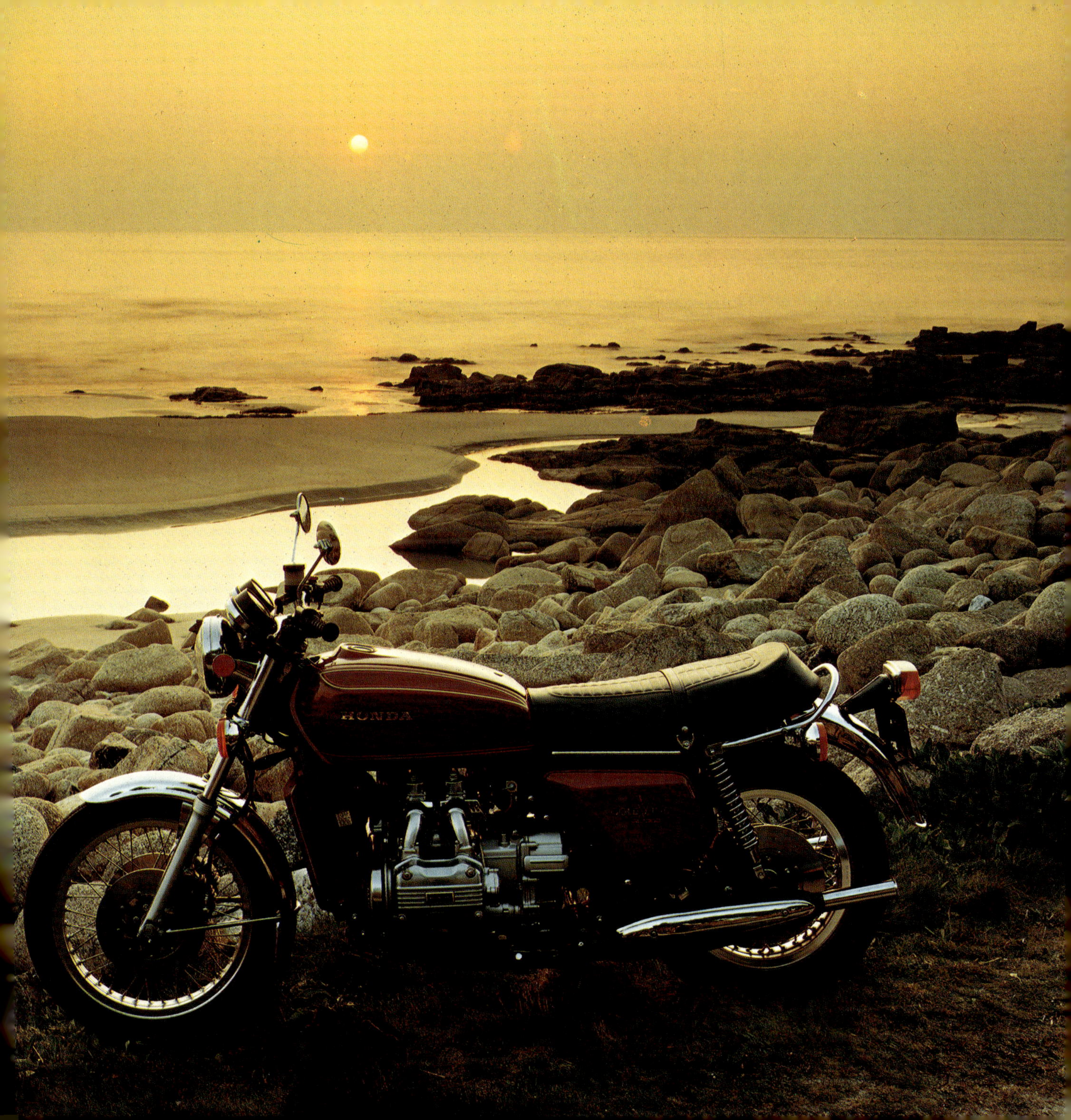
HONDA

VF750 water-cooled, shaft drive motor mounted in a custom-style frame. Tests have shown that, despite its heavy weight, this 113bhp machine will outdrag many bikes away from the lights. One has recorded a 10.90 seconds time for the quarter mile ridden by a professional drag racer.

The CB1000C is a bored out CB900 fitted with shaft drive and a unique transmission that allows the rider to select ten gears. A transfer box switches all normal five speeds through either a low or high ratio for town or freeway use.

A power output of 110bhp is claimed for the CB1100F. Essentially this is just a bored out CB900 with some CB1100R bits fitted, such as the foot rest carriers. It should be capable of something like 135mph.

A real departure for Honda is the American Harley Davidson-style VT750. This is a 45-degree v-twin (like the Harley) but features such modern technology as water-cooling, twin spark plug, three-valve heads, overhead-cams and shaft-drive. It's smooth, too, and tests have shown that this custom-styled bike will average 63mpg – excellent for a 750; but acceleration and top speed are mediocre for the class.

Incredibly the French plan to field a team of air-cooled versions of these machines, specially tuned but mounted in a trail bike frame, for the 3000 miles desert Paris-to-Dakar African rally early in 1984. This bike is known as the XLV750 and is one of the biggest trail bikes ever built.

5 Sporting Bikes

Never content to rest on their laurels Honda have operated a process of continual development in their sporting bikes. In the last 20-odd racing years their four-stroke racers have included single overhead-cam, single-cylinder 50s; OHC twin-cylinder 50s; double overhead-cam 125cc twins; DOHC five-cylinder 125s; DOHC 250s of four and six cylinders; the fabulous 155mph 297cc DOHC six, Mike Hailwood's favourite bike; as well as 350 and 500cc DOHC fours.

By the time they retired from Grand Prix road racing in 1967, they had amassed a record 18 Manufacturers' world titles spanning every class. And the previous year, 1966, won all five solo Manufacturers' classes from 50 to 500cc! In the mid-1970s they came back with an endurance racing 16-valve, DOHC four, displacing close on 1000cc and with a maximum power output of 120bhp making it capable of 160mph.

Honda's moto cross machines have always been single-cylinder two-strokes, but they have pioneered such ideas as single rear shock progressive action suspension systems – Pro Link – that have found their way into racing and road bikes. And they were one of the first manufacturers to come out with long-stroke, 500cc moto cross bikes.

Road-racing Models

Honda's very first racer was a sophisticated 125cc DOHC twin – the RC142. Its maximum power output was around 18.5bhp at 14000rpm, very good for 1959.

Towards the end of 1964 Honda produced their first six-cylinder machine – a fabulous double overhead-cam 250cc racer of fearsome power. The bike revved to something like 18,000rpm and featured a six-speed gearbox. Weight was 247lb, extremely low, and a top speed in the region of 140mph was attainable. This was the bike that took Mike Hailwood to victory in 1966 and 1967, in the World 350cc Championships.

Today, Honda's Grand Prix road-racing machines are both two-stroke and four-stroke. Their most successful machine is the novel v-three NS500 – a 130bhp, water-cooled two-stroke that carried Freddie Spencer to victory in the world in 1983.

overleaf: *Freddie Spencer's mount, and Honda's most successful road-racing machine, the v-three NS500, in action at the 1983 French Grand Prix.* (Photograph courtesy of David Nash.)

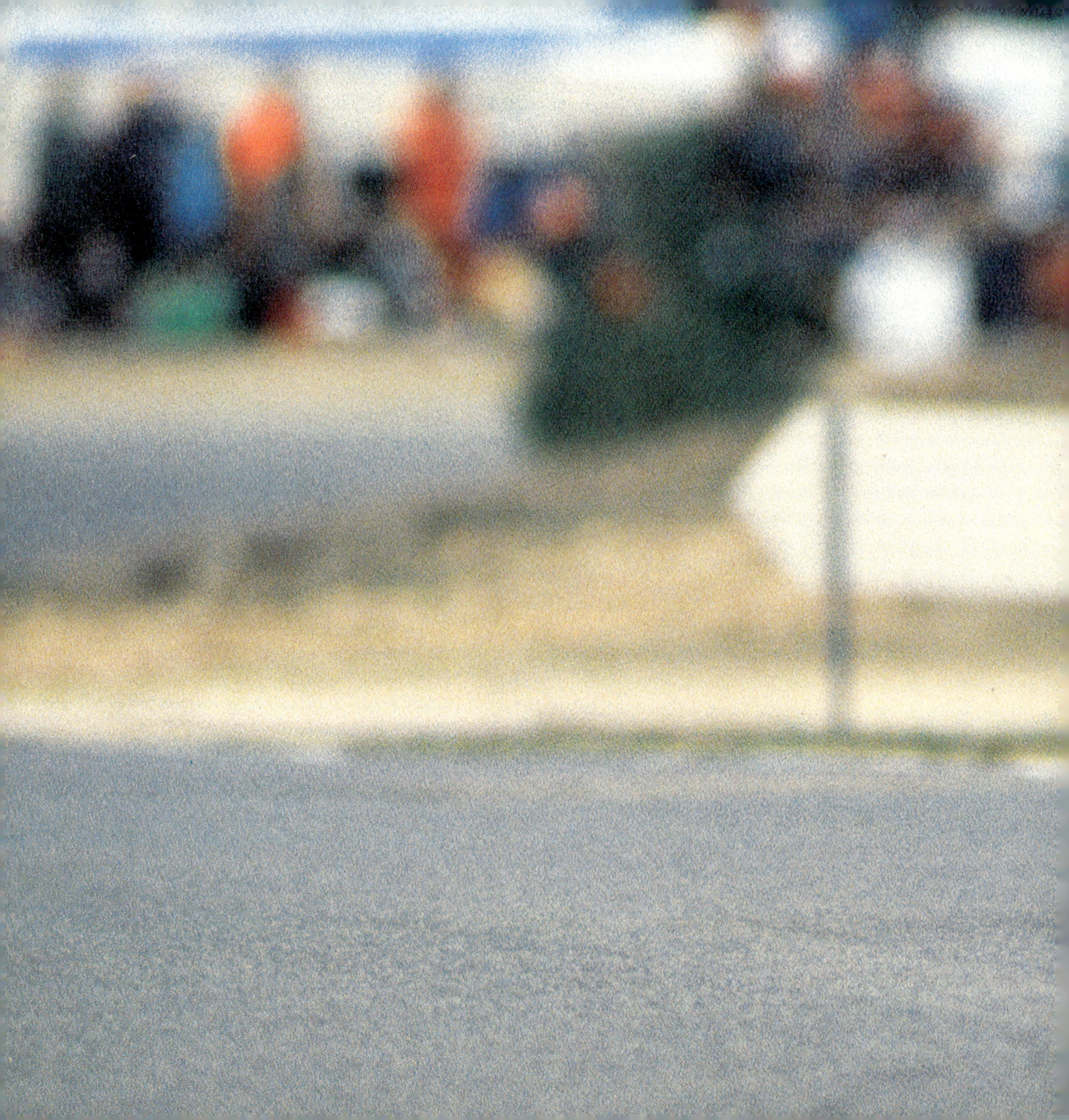

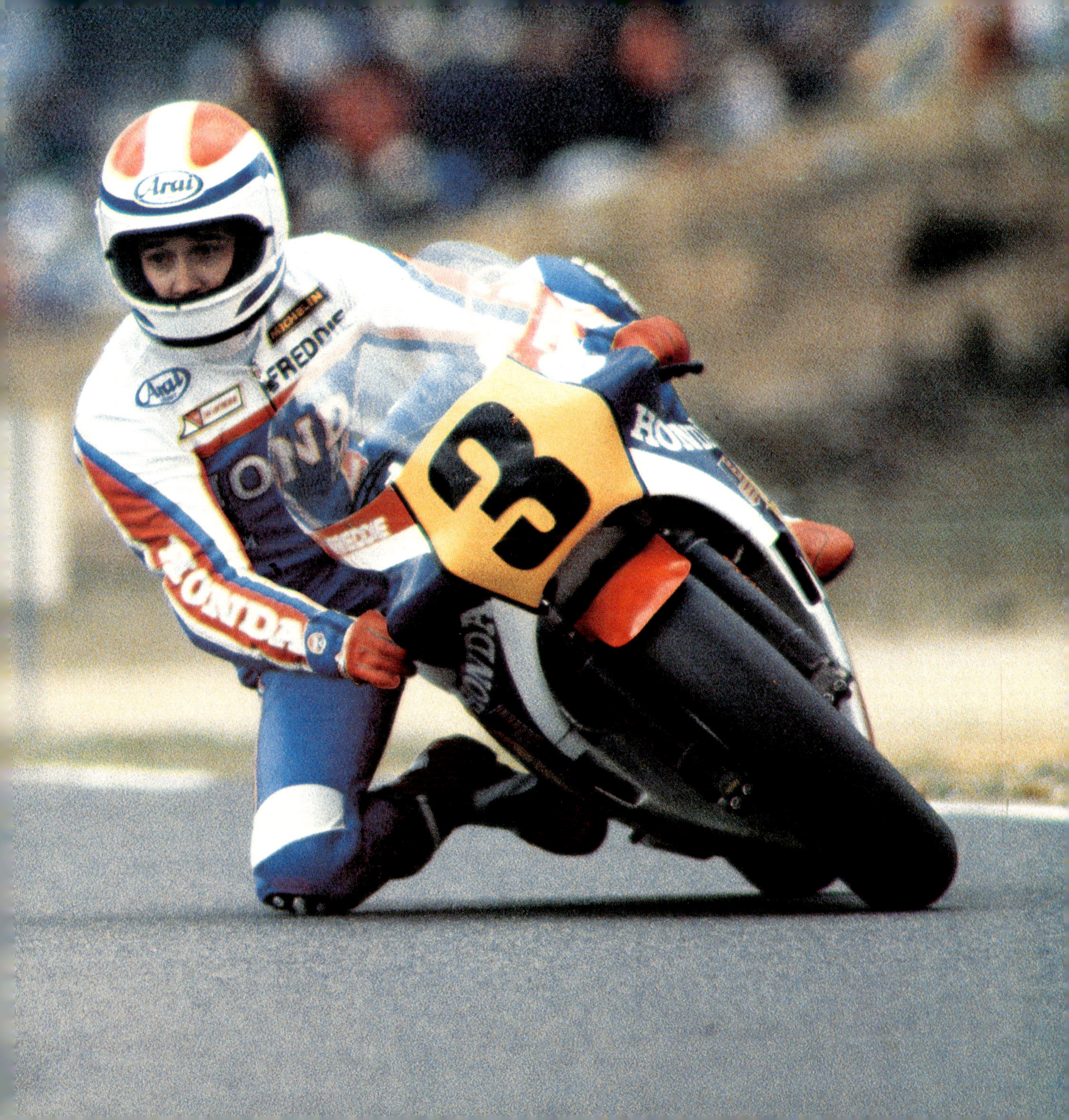
Arai
MICHELIN
FREDDIE
HONDA
3
HONDA
FREDDIE
HONDA

Launched in December 1981, the NS has an engine configuration with the two rear cylinders parallel and upright and a third pointing forward at an angle of 112 degrees. It's a low bike – 44½in. to the top of the petrol tank – thanks to the compact engine. The box-section twin-loop aluminiun frame has a Pro Link single shock rear end and telescopic front forks have an anti-dive arrangement built in.

Honda's novel v-four, the NR500, has all but been retired from the Grands Prix after failing to score any World Championship points. An interesting bike from a technical viewpoint, the engine has 'long round' pistons (rectangular with rounded ends). It's believed to have no less than eight valves per cylinder and twin con rods to stop the pistons rocking.

There will be three big v-four four-strokes competing around the world in 1984. The World Endurance and Tourist Trophy Formula One rounds will be contested with the RS750R, a 140bhp monster capable of over 160mph. In the U.S.A., where they have different regulations, works riders Mike Baldwin and Steve Wise will race a works version of the VF750 roadster in their Superbike events.

The latest version of the 1982 RS1000RW v-four Daytona racer, rumoured to churn out 150bhp, will also appear in some U.S. events.

The RS750, like all the v-fours, has double overhead-cams, four valves per cylinder and water cooling. Its dry weight is claimed to be as low as 263lb.

The riders who'll be competing in the

Honda's range of sporting production bikes runs from the schoolboy CR80R moto crosser . . .

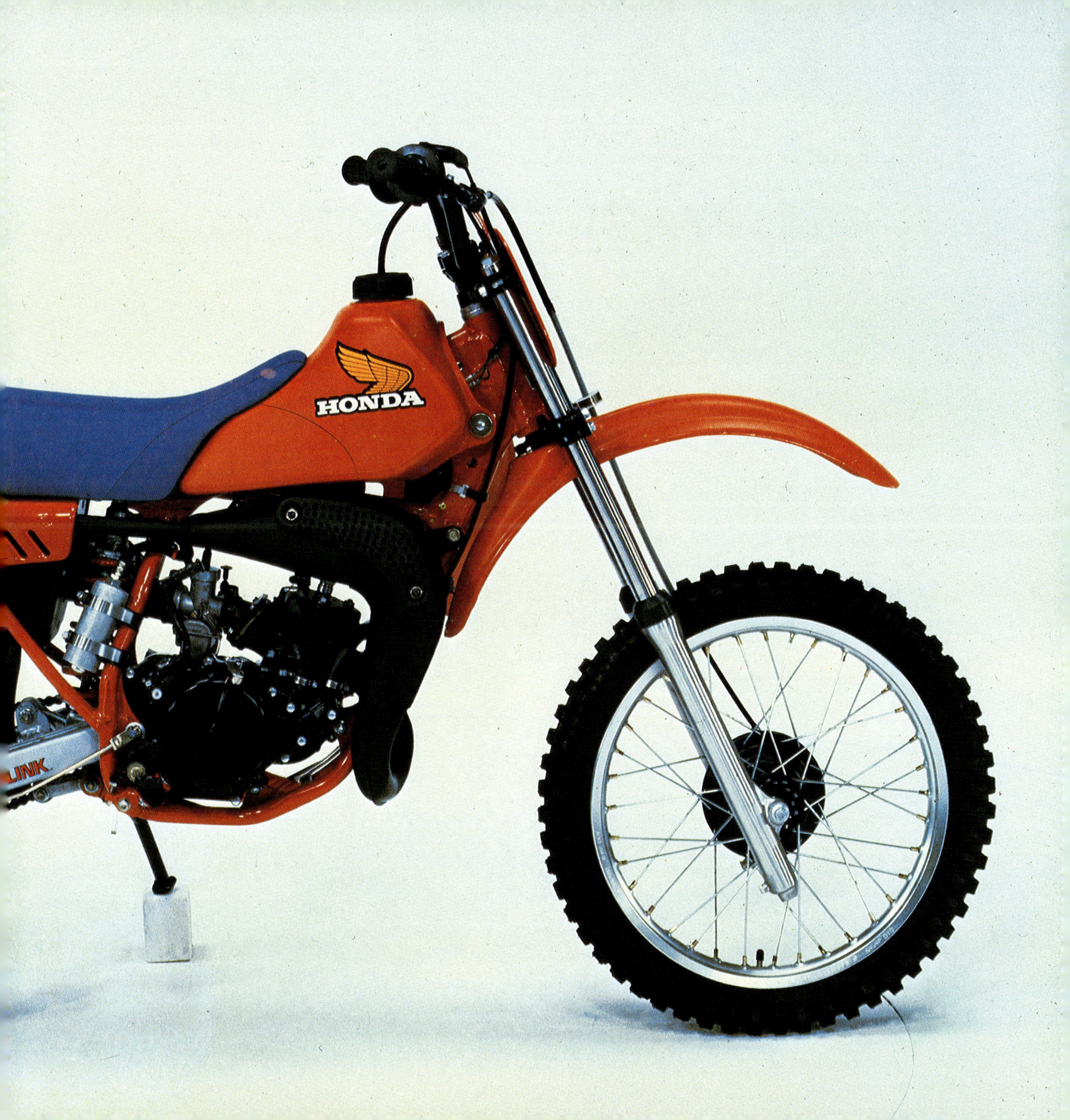
HONDA
LINK

endurance series of 24-hour events will be headed by Frenchman Raymond Roche.

All the v-fours, like the roadsters, have a twin loop frame and Pro Link rear end. Front wheels are all 16in. in diameter.

Moto Cross

Currently Honda produce just two true works moto crossers: the RC500M as campaigned by

. . . to the incredibly powerful CR480R, Graham Noyce replica moto crosser.

Graham Noyce and André Malherbe, and the RC250M.

Both are reed valve induction and are conventionally piston ported, but the 250 is water-cooled. An exciting development for 1984 is a water-cooled 500cc machine that will be raced experimentally in some international events. Water-cooling is almost unheard of in large capacity machines.

The 500 has a long stroke for better torque, and is rumoured to produce around 65bhp at

The ATC185 is a multi-purpose three-wheeler, useful on farms and all kinds of rough terrain.

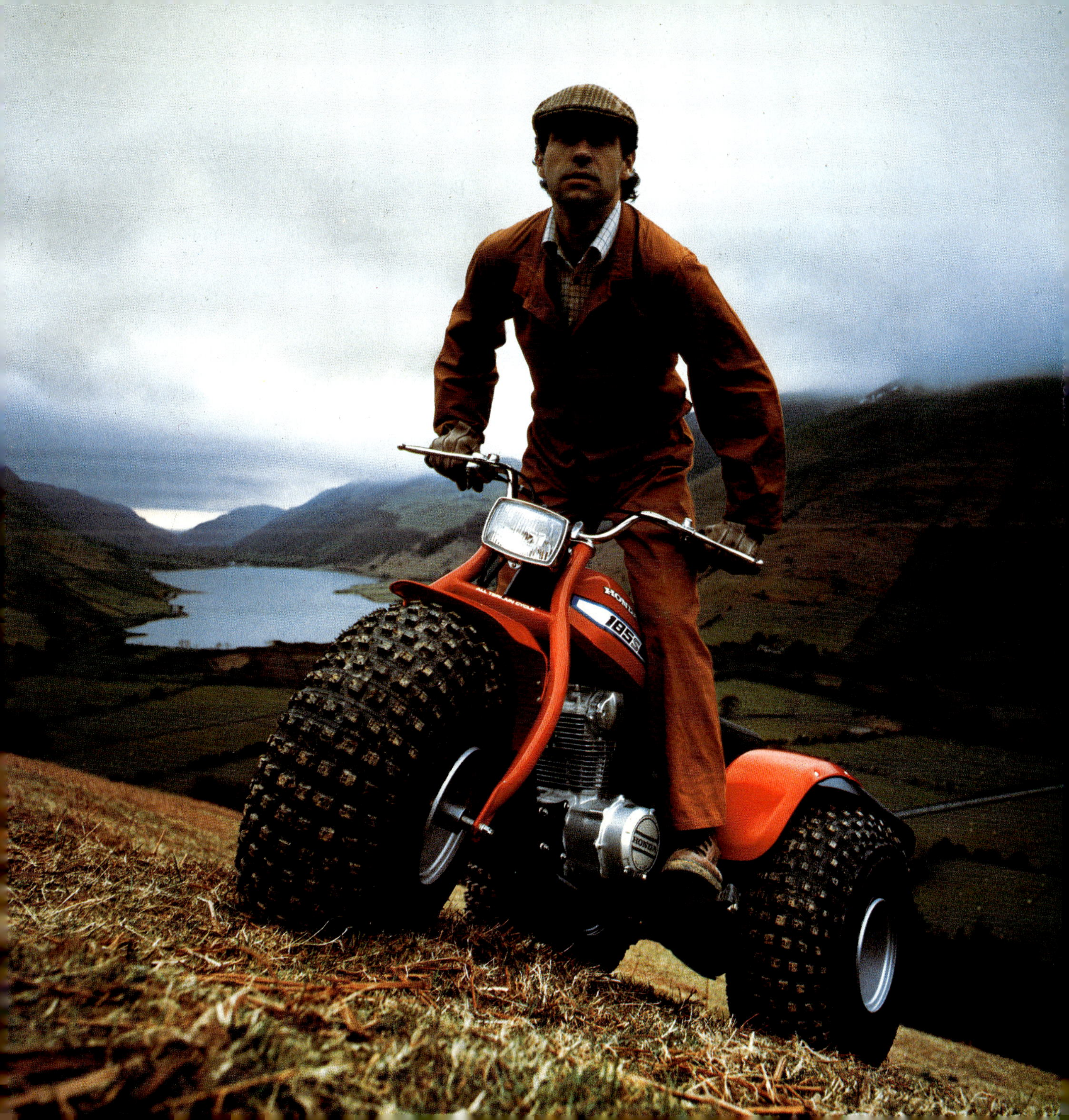
185S
ALL TERRAIN CYCLE
HONDA

7000rpm. The 250 produces in the region of 45bhp. Both have over a foot of suspension travel front and rear and the Pro Link system at the rear gives a progressive spring rate.

Massive 44mm diameter fork tubes are fitted at the front to prevent flexing. Careful use of light alloys and plastics have allowed Honda to keep the weight of the 500 down to something like 221lb dry.

Trials

World trials champion Eddy Lejeune will campaign a works four-stroke single RS3607T trials bike in the 1984 championships. Designed to produce maximum torque at low revs, the RS360 is air-cooled and mounted in a very light frame. The total weight is only 206lb dry!

Production Machines

Honda's range of sporting production bikes runs all the way from the CR80R – a water-cooled, high-performance, schoolboy moto cross machine – all the way up to the massively powerful CR480R Graham Noyce replica moto crosser. In between there's a whole range of moto cross and enduro machinery, even a racing All Terrain Cycle (ATC) 250cc three-wheeler.

The moto cross range starts at the CR80R; there's a 125cc machine – the water-cooled CR125R; a water-cooled 250, and, of course, the air-cooled CR480R.

All are two-stroke and all have Honda's own Pro Link rear suspension for ironing out the fiercest bumps.

The enduro range are street-legal, with lights, and are all single-cylinder, single overhead-cam four-strokes. Smallest is the XR200R; biggest is the XR500R; though a 600cc machine – the XL600R – is available in the U.S.A. and elsewhere as a desert racer. All have four-valve heads with the valves arranged in a radical fashion for better performance, and all have Honda's famous Pro Link rear suspension chassis. (The XR500 is not available in Britain.)

In addition, Honda do two off-road children's fun bikes: the Z50R and QR50. Both are suitable for kids to ride under adult supervision off-road. The Z50 uses a variant of the ubiquitous, 50cc, OHC, scooterette engine; while the QR50 is a two-stroke.

Honda invented the term ATC for All Terrain Cycles and their three-wheeler range is second to none with six machines available in the U.K. All but the racing 250 are single-cylinder four-strokes and ideally suited for kids and adults to ride. Some are even being modified for use by the disabled.

Smallest is the ATC 70 with a tiny (scooterette-type) engine; there are 110 and 185cc versions and a powerful 200cc machine, the ATC200E, which is being used by farmers for all kinds of hard work. A more sporty 200 is the ATC200X which is designed as a racer and has a manual clutch and front disc brake. The ATC250R is raced in Britain and the U.S.A. It features an air-cooled, moto cross, two-stroke engine, five-speed manual transmission, and moto cross-type suspension, including the rear Pro Link system.

6 Star Riders

Freddie Spencer

'Fast' Freddie Spencer is Honda's first ever World 500cc Champion – and he's only 22 years old!

A racing professional since his teens Spencer has gained quite a following in Europe after just one full year on the Grand Prix circus. But after a successful career in the America he has had no problems sorting out the European scene. He says, 'The hardest thing is not knowing what to expect when you arrive in a new place. I was a little homesick at first, but it's not that bad because I don't let it affect my riding.'

Fast Freddie piloted his ultra quick NS500 triple to victory in the 1983 World road-race Championship with a maturity that belied his years. He battled all season long against fellow countryman Kenny Roberts, a Yamaha veteran nine years his senior, but just pipped him at the post in the final Grand Prix. There were no breakdowns, no problems – it was a masterly performance. Spencer turned down some lucrative offers in favour of racing Honda's new, unproven v-three NS500 two-stroke in 1982 and many felt he should have stayed at home racing established Honda superbike machinery. But he has no regrets: 'I've been racing so long in the 'States that it had become like going to work as a not as popular with the crowds. Over here the enormous crowds and their enthusiasm can't help but motivate you. I doubt if I could just go back and race in the 'States again.'

Freddie was just 20 years old when he won his first Grand Prix in Belgium in 1982 – two years later he'd taken his (and Honda's) first individual World 500cc road-race Championship.

Marco Lucchinelli

Italian Marco Lucchinelli is a man who loves road racing. He loves the excitement, the adrenalin rush of high speed action, and he loves the atmosphere of being around other racers and racing machines. Married (to Paola) and with two children, the Grands Prix are very much a family affair for Lucchinelli because he takes his family everywhere with him.

An excitable, lean live-wire of a man Lucchinelli, like most Italians, talks with his hands and can be seen around the paddock with his helmet perched on the top of his head, leaving his hands free for conversation.

World Champion in 1981 on a Suzuki,

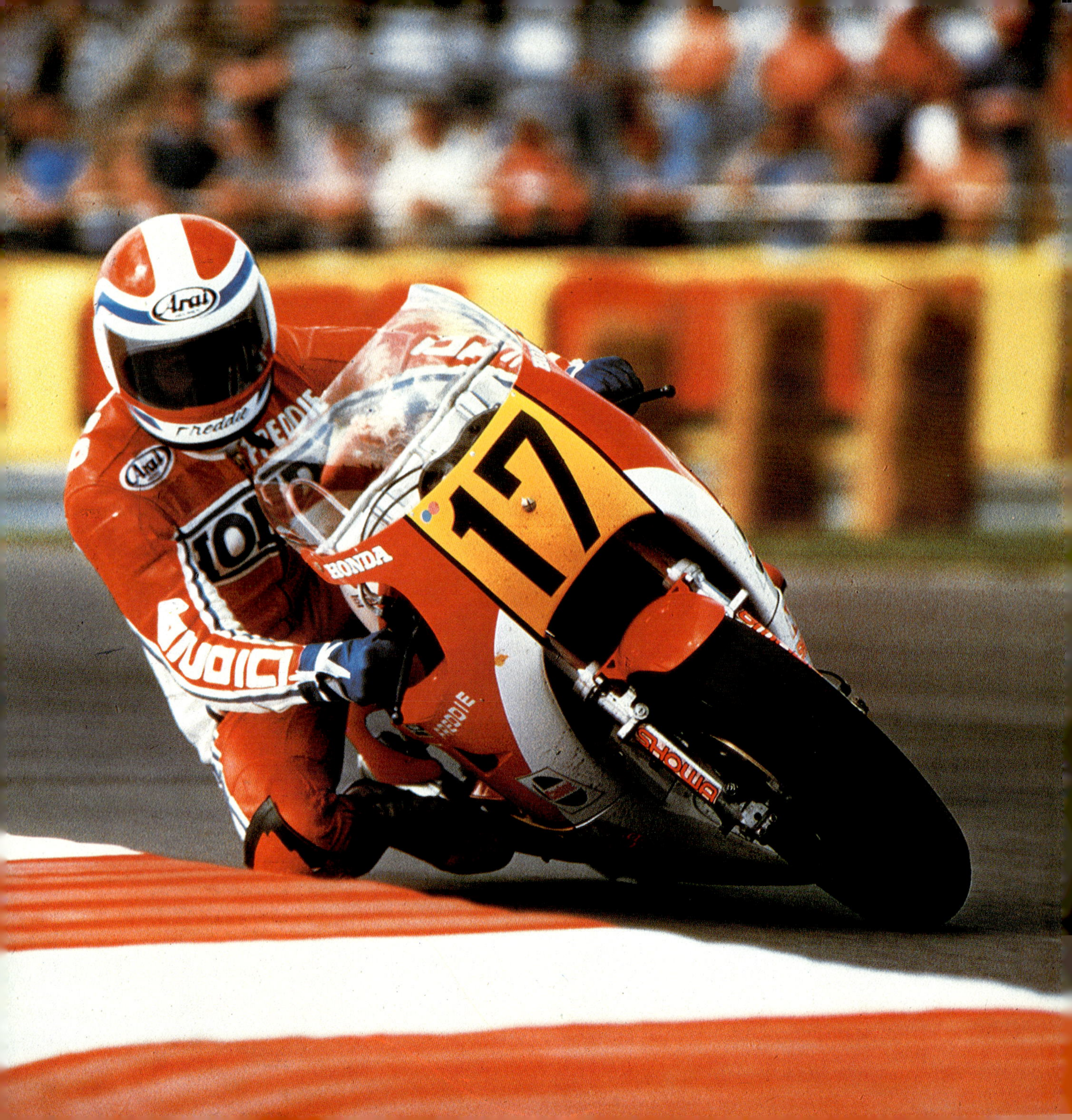
Arai
Freddie
17
HONDA

Lucchinelli had a dreadful début year with Honda in 1982 crashing and injuring himself and finishing in eighth place in the 500cc.

But he's determined to make his luck change. He does not believe in sitting back, waiting for things to happen. 'I *want* to win the World Championship again, desperately', he says, 'I'm determined to make my luck change. When I won the World Championship I started a new phase in my life. Now I am no longer World Champion I have started another phase in my life.'

André Malherbe

Good-looking, tousle-haired, Belgian André Malherbe set a difficult act to follow when he won the International 125cc moto cross Championship in 1974 as a teenager. But he didn't let that early success go to his head and, unlike his protégé Graham Noyce, he progressed up to the 250cc Championship for a couple of years before switching to the 500cc class in 1978.

Riding with a maturity that belied his age he finished sixth on an Austrian KTM machine. 'My father helped me get started in moto cross', he syas, 'he ran a bike shop and prepared my early 125cc Zundapp machines. But I wasn't forced to race, you understand.'

In 1979, the year Noyce won the world title, Malherbe joined the official Honda world 500cc Grand Prix team and raced brilliantly to third place in the Championship. There were no team orders or anything like that – both Noyce and Malherbe raced to win. 'I admire Graham (Noyce) as a competitor and he is my friend,' he says. 'We get on well and that's good.'

With Noyce stuck for luck in 1980, Malherbe raced brilliantly to his first world title. He did it again in 1981 to give Honda three world 500cc titles in a row.

A married man, Malherbe, like Noyce has had a good run of success and doesn't feel that he has anything left to prove. But he's still eager for success and, like all Belgian moto crossers, would love to beat fellow countryman Joel Robert's record tally of six world titles. 'Yes of course that would be fantastic', he readily admits, 'just give me a little more time!'

Graham Noyce

When Graham Noyce won the World 500cc moto cross Championship for Honda in 1979 he was just 22 years old. That made him the youngest-ever man to win this prestigious title. If that makes him a prodigy, then it's a label he's well used to. He has been racing since he was 10, won the British schoolboy Championship at 14 and the British senior Championship at 18.

It's difficult for Noyce, now 26 years old, to live down his reputation of being a child star, and even more difficult to live up to expectations. What more can you do when you have already reached the top at just 22? 'It's difficult staying at the top', he says. 'It's something you've got to work at.' And work is something Noyce is used to.

Freddie Spencer in action at Silverstone on his NR500.

61

At 22 Graham Noyce was the youngest to win the 500cc moto cross Championship.

He has not had the best of luck since he won the world title: he has been dogged with injuries, crashes and sheer bad luck, and has fought back every time.

He has, however, no thoughts of quitting. 'I feel I'm getting back to my old form again', he says. 'I'm working very hard to keep myself fit and I'm taking a positive view.'

He used to be labelled headstrong, but time and success have mellowed him. Now he takes a more philosophic view, a more mature approach to victory.

Noyce quit Britain several years ago for tax reasons; his earnings were – and still are – in the super tax bracket. But now he lives with his new wife Pam and her two children at a smart rambling home in the Sussex downs. He's happy now and settled. But he still wants that 500cc world crown again. 'You bet I do', he says. 'I'm just as hungry for victory as I've always been. You just watch me go!'

Eddy Lejeune

Bespectacled Belgian Eddy Lejeune didn't just win the World trials Championship last year – he completely dominated it. But it's a little ironic that Honda should triumph in this particular branch of motor-cycle sport because their efforts in trials are just a drop in the ocean compared to their million pounds' involvement in 500cc Grand Prix road racing.

Despite Honda's relative lack of interest, Lejeune triumphed with ease on a four-stroke, single-cylinder machine that is virtually unchanged since its début several years ago.

Lejeune is something of a child prodigy. Just 21 years old he has been riding since he was 13 and knows no other trade. A youthful-looking man from Liège, where his parents run a plastic bottle making plant, he speaks only French and Flemish and is something of a loner. Married to Dominique, he loves to talk about trials: 'it's my life . . . it always has been', he says 'I don't know what I'll do if, and when, I retire. That's not something I think about.' He is a talented rider who makes few mistakes and has an uncanny knack of picking the neatest course through difficult and unfamiliar sections (a skill that infuriates his older, more experienced opponents).

Despite Honda's relative lack of interest in trials riding, compared with their huge investment in Grand Prix road racing, Belgian Eddy Lejeune dominated the World trials Championship in 1983 on a Honda mount.

Index

Alloys 47, 58
Alternator 36
Amigo moped 14, 15
Anti-dive suspension 36, 38, 41, 42
Aspencade 48
ATC 14, 58
A-Type 7, 10
Auto Bai 10

Baldwin, Mike 54
Benly 10, 11, 12
Brakes, linked 48
B-Type 10

C50 15, 20
C71 12
C72 12
Camino 17
CB77 13, 14
CB92 12, 13
CB125T 24, 27
CB250 14
CB400F 34
CB750 14, 38, 39, 40, 41
CB900 41, 42
CB1100R 47, 50
CBX550 39
CBX1000 47
CG125 23
Clock 41
Clutch, hydraulic 38
Commuting 15
Comstar wheel 28
Counterbalance shafts 34
Cub 10, 11, 20
CX500 36, 43
CX650 38, 47

Daytona 41, 54
Decompressor 28, 30
Dirt track 36
Disc brake 39
Discs, inboard 32
Discs, ventilated 47
Dream 10, 11, 12
D-Type 10

Econopower 20
Elsinore 14
Endurance racing 40, 41, 56
E-Type 10, 11
Eurosport 38

Eurostyling 28
Exports 10
Express moped 17, 20

Farm bike 24
Flat track racing 36
FT500 36
Fuel injection 43
Fun bikes 58

Gold Wing 14, 47, 48
Grands Prix 40, 51, 59, 62

Hailwood, Mike 51
Hamamatsu 7
Harley Davidson 50
Honda, Soichiro 7, 10, 11

Isle of Man 11, 54

J-Type 12
Juno 10

KTM 61

Lead 22
Learners 12, 27
Lejeune, Eddy 58, 62
Liège, Belgium 40, 62
Lucchinelli 59, 61

Magna, VF1100 48
Malherbe, André 56, 61
Mann, Dick 40
Melody 20
Moto cross 51, 56
MTX125 24
MTX200 27
MVX250 32

Nighthawk 38
Noise regulations 35
Novio 20
Noyce, Graham 56, 58, 61, 62
NR500 54
NS500 32, 54, 59

Paris–Dakar Rally 50
Plastics 41, 47, 58
Pressed-steel frame 12, 27
Progressive action suspension 51

Racers 51
RC142 51
RC250 56, 58
RC500 56, 58
Radio 48
Reed valve 56
Robert, Joel 61
Roberts, Kenny 59
Roche, Raymond 56
RS750R 54
RS1000 54

Schoolboy moto cross 58, 61
Scooterette 11
Scooters 15, 20
Shadow 37
Spacy 22
Spencer, Freddie 51, 59
Stop-watch 41
Super Dream 28
Superbike 14, 38, 39, 48

Telescopic front suspension 13
Three-valve head 13
Tourist trophy 54
Trailbike 23
Transfer-box 50
Trials riding 62
Triumph Trident 39
Turbo 38, 43, 47
Twiggy 17
Two-stroke 7, 15

V65 48
Valves, hydraulic 38
Valves, reed 56
VF750 41
VT250 30
VT500 37
VT750 48

XL125 23
XL250 28, 32
XL500 36
XL600R 58
XLV750 50

Wet sump lubrication 28
Wise, Steve 54

Yamaha 32, 36

Zundapp 61